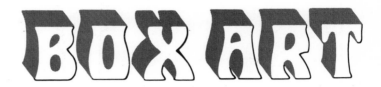

BOX ART

Assemblage
and Construction

BY DONA Z. MEILACH

CROWN PUBLISHERS, INC., NEW YORK

Books by Dona Z. Meilach in Crown's Arts and Crafts Series:

COLLAGE AND ASSEMBLAGE
    with Elvie Ten Hoor
CONTEMPORARY ART WITH WOOD
CONTEMPORARY BATIK AND TIE-DYE
CONTEMPORARY STONE SCULPTURE
DIRECT METAL SCULPTURE
    with Donald Seiden
MACRAMÉ ACCESSORIES
MACRAMÉ: CREATIVE DESIGN IN KNOTTING
A MODERN APPROACH TO BASKETRY WITH FIBERS AND GRASSES
PAPIER-MÂCHÉ ARTISTRY
SOFT SCULPTURE AND OTHER SOFT ART FORMS
SCULPTURE CASTING
    with Dennis Kowal

Also by Dona Z. Meilach:

ACCENT ON CRAFTS
THE ARTIST'S EYE
COLLAGE AND FOUND ART
    with Elvie Ten Hoor
CONTEMPORARY LEATHER: ART AND ACCESSORIES
CREATING ART FROM ANYTHING
CREATING ART FROM FIBERS AND FABRICS
HOW TO CREATE DESIGN
    with Jay Hinz and Bill Hinz
CREATING WITH PLASTER
CREATIVE STITCHERY
    with Lee Erlin Snow
MAKING CONTEMPORARY RUGS AND WALL HANGINGS
PAPERCRAFT
PRINTMAKING
WEAVING OFF-LOOM
    with Lee Erlin Snow

Library of Congress Cataloging in Publication Data

Meilach, Dona Z
    Box art: assemblage and construction.

    Bibliography: p.
    Includes index.
    1. Boxes. 2. Boxes in art. I. Title.
NK3665.M44   745.5   74-20513
ISBN 0-517-51620-9
ISBN 0-517-51621-7 pbk.

Contents

Dedicated to:

Gordon Wagner, Los Angeles, California,
who stimulated and instigated
the creation of this
book

and to:

The memory and creativity of
Joseph Cornell

Acknowledgments

A sincere thank-you to all of the artists who contributed photos of their work and invited me to photograph their boxes. I am especially grateful to the following for their detailed development of specific demonstrations: Judith Citrin, Wilmette, Illinois; Sabato Fiorello, Los Angeles, California; John Schroeder, Los Angeles, California; Arlene Seitzinger, Portage, Indiana; and Gordon Wagner, Los Angeles, California.

I am deeply appreciative to the cooperation of the galleries and museums who have provided photos: Jacqueline Anhalt Gallery, Los Angeles; Galeria Bonino, Ltd., New York; Louis K. Meisel Gallery, New York; Orlando Gallery, Encino, California; Stefanotty Gallery, New York; Allan Stone Gallery, New York; The Art Institute of Chicago, and the Museum of Contemporary Art, Chicago.

A special thanks to my son, Allen Meilach, who produced the line drawings and to my husband, Dr. Melvin Meilach, who assisted with the photography, travel arrangements, and interviews.

I want to acknowledge the work of the various photographers whose credits accompany the photos and to Ben Lavitt, Astra Photo Service, Inc., Chicago, for his continuing interest in the photographic reproductions needed for a top quality book.

Dona Z. Meilach
Palos Heights, Illinois

Note: All photos by Dona and Mel Meilach unless otherwise credited.

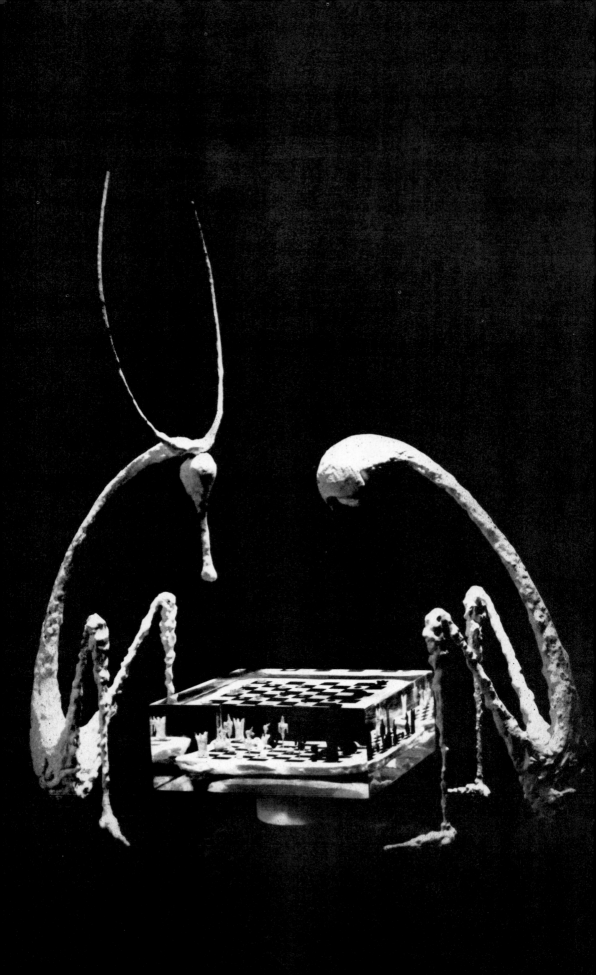

The Box Environment

ARTISTS ARE CONSISTENTLY INVOLVED WITH AND STIMULATED by their environment. They take from it, relate to it, create with it in many ingenious manners. One recent and rapidly emerging manner is that of the box as a container for an assemblage of sculptural images. As this activity has appeared on the contemporary art scene, finding a suitable name or "umbrella" under which to classify the results has been elusive. Such exhibits titled SMALL ENVIRONMENTS or SMALL IMAGES really didn't describe what the viewer might expect.

Interviews with the artists involved consistently emphasized the concept of the box as an environment. Many artists referred to themselves as "box makers," or "image makers." One described himself as "an assemblage artist who likes to work with the box form"; others used the term "sculptural collage." Regardless of the appellation, all agreed that the box form had a universality. Within it could be captured a concept, imagery, symbolism, and the entire array of human activities. To all of them the box represented an essence of a real or imaginary larger world. Therefore, the title for this Chapter, THE BOX ENVIRONMENT appeared to be most suitable.

One artist succinctly summed up the attitude of many: "We begin in the enclosed space of the womb, we live out our lives in boxes: rooms, automobiles, homes and, finally, caskets. The box represents the microcosm of man's existence."

◀

KING AND QUEEN PLAYING CHESS. Jephan de Villiers. 1973. A hand-carved chess set is embedded in a plastic box. A sculptured king and queen complete the environmental setting.

Courtesy, Prudhoe Gallery, London

SOAP BUBBLE SET. Joseph Cornell. Bubble pipes, goblets, glass balls, conch shell, and other objects in a box are combined with a drawing and a printed sheet from a French book about the planets. Cornell used objects and images that contrast with one another.

Collection, The Art Institute of Chicago

It is impossible to pinpoint the first box and box maker. Several important artists have been fascinated with its potential for many years. Joseph Cornell's work undoubtedly prevails and is the foundation on which current box makers have based much of their inspiration. Cornell, originally a painter, began assembling objects in boxes in the 1930s and steadily produced box forms until his death in 1972.

Cornell's early boxes were literal and the objects within them were everyday items such as brass rings, clay soap bubble pipes, goblets, and sand. As he matured, his environments consisted of a range of incongruous images assembled much as a poet assembles words and rhythms. They became visual metaphors with a private, yet deeply effective, poetic congruity of their own. Commonplace objects were often combined with maps of the heavens or with prints of master art works. In each box there is a wonder and mystery combined with details and pleasurable surprises. Viewing the boxes, trying to decipher the metaphors, is completely absorbing whether or not one is aware of Cornell's exact meanings. They suggest windows to a small world that existed in the artist's dreams and mind.

Other artists have produced box forms, but not as consistently as did Cornell. Arthur Dove's early assemblages were created in a shadow box frame. Arman's box forms contain "accumulations" and

SPACE OBJECT BOX. Joseph Cornell. 1959. 9½ inches high, 15 inches wide, 3¾ inches deep. Cornell's boxes appear as games he played to place unrelated objects with similar configurations in different planes so the shapes would relate to each other.

Courtesy, Allan Stone Gallery, New York

are often titled that way, for example, "Accumulation of Teapots." Several teapots are cut in half or fragmented and assembled within the box. The result is a sculptural statement using the medium of our "consumption-mad modern society, its junk and rejected odd objects."

Lucas Samaras's boxes are wildly different from one another and from those of Cornell or Arman. Unlike Cornell, whose interest is in window-frame boxes, Samaras became intrigued by boxes when he realized he could cover the exteriors with something. Says Samaras, "My first couple of boxes were painted with black or silver, but when I started covering them with pins, wool and jewels, I subverted their geometry . . . buried it . . . and gave myself an opportunity to use and introduce ordinary yet strange substances."

In the beginning Samaras outfitted a few second-hand boxes, but now most of them are made to order. He is concerned with a relationship of objects and ideas. He develops these with contrasts of textures, with handmade and organic materials, and with contrasting colors. He may use yarn, stuffed birds, sparkling crystals, tacks, pins, razor blades, pieces of rock, X rays of hands and heads, and photographic portraits of himself. Some of the pieces appear menacing; many have erotic overtones.

Sometimes Samaras's boxes give the impression that the artist

BOX # 53. (Closed and open
views.) Lucas Samaras. 1966. 12
inches wide, 9 inches deep. Wood
box with multicolored yarn, stuffed
birds, tape measure, natural crystal,
metal ore.
*Courtesy, The Art Institute of
Chicago*

suffered from some *horror vacuii* that compelled him to fill in every
available space. The interiors may be filled with tiny compartments,
drawers, recesses, each occupied with something: pencils, seashells,
tacks, and transparent objects. Some depend on shadows, mirrors,
and razzle-dazzle for their impact.

A group of West Coast artists has been working with box forms
for about a decade. Ed Keinholz, Wallace Berman, Ben Talbert,

ATTIC ANGEL. Joan Hall. 1971. 4 inches high, 7½ inches wide, 3 inches deep. A tiny box becomes the setting for a scene filled with nostalgia and personal symbolism.

Courtesy, artist

George Herms, Fred Masson, Bettye Saar, and Gordon Wagner were early proponents. Their first pieces were assemblages dealing with social and political criticism, sexual fantasy, and a private mythology. In their latter works, the imagery altered and mellowed.

Gordon Wagner's box environments are now avant-garde and arresting in their scope and variety. He portrays mystical, surrealistic imagery that conveys meaning and a deep involvement with the aspects of life that affect the artist and his larger environment. Wagner refers to his boxes as "magic" because they transform a vision to an unreal or real situation. They are like scenes on the stage of a mini-theater where mind dramas and micro-comedies are performed. His boxes are essentially constructions, not assemblages. Almost every piece is handmade; only occasionally will he incorporate a found object. The interiors may be movable so that they carry out the drama and change the scene just as actors might do on a stage. Says Wagner, "I find the world quite ugly, banal, and trite. Too real. I like to capture a vision, or a small part of the world that still has some mystery to it, and encase it forever in a box."

BEDROOM. Michael Hurson. 1972. 6½ inches high, 14⅝ inches wide, 9⅝ inches deep. Monotone woods carefully crafted reveal a stark environment that is reminiscent of the paintings by Edward Hopper. They suggest life; yet they are immobile, tranquil, and surreal.
Courtesy, Museum of Contemporary Art, Chicago

➤

CHANCE. Gordon Wagner. 1972. 16 inches high, 12 inches wide, 5 inches deep. Magical dream images with playful illusions are indigenous to Wagner's boxes. A die, magnified behind a lens, is reflected in the triple mirror. When the interior portion of the box is turned around, another composition appears.
Courtesy, Sylvan Simone Gallery, West Los Angeles

Box makers work with a variety of imagery, symbolism, and realism achieved by any means conceivable: found objects, handmade items, mirrors, shadows, fragmented forms, layers of glass or plastic, transparent images, collage, painting, and the entire array of techniques and devices brought from other art forms. Their philosophies are as varied as the artists, yet they have similarities: dissatisfaction with the world, satire, dream images, nostalgia, love, joy, sex, and so forth.

Whatever the stimulus, the box environment has piqued innovators and followers. It holds tantalizing promise for additional exploration by the fertile imaginations of creators and viewers. This first compilation of the activity of box makers heralds, without doubt, the emergence of an additional branch on the verdant tree of contemporary art.

The Basic Box and
Other Materials

THE BASIC BOX USED TO CONTAIN THE ENVIRONMENTS MAY
have served another purpose at one time or it may be constructed by
the artist. A box that previously had a specific identity can be a
challenge to the box maker who likes to discover ordinary objects
and give them a new life as art. Such boxes have potential because
they are abundant and their variety in size, shape, materials, hardware, and other elements is unlimited.

Anything from a tiny plastic pillbox to a wooden cigar box to
fine lacquered oriental boxes is used in the examples shown. Study
the boxes closely to determine what their origins might have been,
then begin to see potential in boxes used in every industry and
service such as those on barbers' counters, jewelry cases, drug
supplies, crates, packing boxes, drawers, and cutlery dividers. Seek
boxes of wood, plastic, glass, mirrors, fabric, ceramic, fiberboard.
When necessary, think of how you can alter them to serve your need.
You might want to attach a frame by adding a glass panel and molding, and to add compartments or shelves. You can collage a box
bottom, back, or exterior or fit it with pieces of cut mirror.

To construct boxes to your own specifications and designs you
will require basic carpenter's tools and methods for joining the corners. The most common wood joints are illustrated. A wood box
can have a stationary pane of glass on one or two sides; it may have
doors that open and shut, or a lid. It can be embellished with hardware and decorative moldings including a variety of pre-cut shapes
available from a lumber dealer.

Boxes may be viewed from the front or opened from the top.
They can be like magician's boxes with false bottoms and compartments that can contain a wealth of surprises.

FINISHING   A wood box may be left in its natural state or treated
as the wood in a fine piece of sculpture or furniture. Depending on

14

The basic box may be an assortment of those used for other purposes and "recycled" as an artistic statement. Or you can make a box from new or used lumber. Basic box making tools required are: hammer, nails, drills, saws, rulers, screwdrivers, T-square, clamps, corner reinforcements, sandpaper, miter box, paint brushes and paint finishes: stains, varnish, paints.

the quality and type of wood (pine, oak, redwood, and so forth), it may be stained or oiled to bring out the natural finish and then protected with gloss or matte varnish. It can be painted one color or decorated with many using household paints or artists' acrylic colors.

OTHER MATERIALS The majority of the boxes incorporate found objects and these can be infinitely varied. The box maker must be a collector and squirrel away assorted objects culled from every possible source: junk heaps, rummage and garage sales, collectors and others. Old magazines and new art papers can provide collage materials. To adhere the materials to the boxes, you will need hammers, nails, tacks, and in most cases, glue. Different materials require different glue properties. You can consult the Glue Chart on page 94 for specific glues to use.

   Ceramic boxes and miscellaneous parts can be made of clay and fired in a kiln. You can also mold objects from papier-mâché, self-hardening clays, and bread dough. You can build armatures for the soft materials; you can carve some objects directly from clay, wood, and plaster.

Glass and plastic are available in different thicknesses and are used for enclosing the box, framing, shelving and dividers. Mirrors are important for illusions. Glass and mirror are available from hardware stores and glass dealers: they can be cut to order or you can cut pieces with a good quality glass cutter. Investigate the new mirror-finish Plexiglas that is lightweight, easy to cut, and will not crack or break.

Collect old lenses from your local optometrist who usually throws them out. Cultivate any source you need to supply the materials you want—a cigar store for cigar boxes, a director of an aviary for feathers, a butcher for bones, and so forth. You must be as creative at securing your materials as you are at using them.

Butt joint   **Rabbet joint**   **Miter joint**

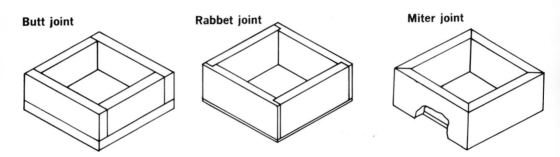

A box usually requires five pieces of wood joined at the corners by simple carpentry joints. The back, or bottom, can be placed over or within the side members. It may remain uncovered or it can have glass on the front or on the back and front.

Butt   **Dowel**

The *butt,* or plain, joint is the simplest to make, but not very strong. It is made by overlapping one piece over the other and nailing the two together. All ends should be perfectly square. Do not use too many nails or they will weaken the joint. If a box will not be handled too much and if a glass frame and front molding are added, the butt joint can be satisfactory. Use glue in the joint along with the nails or screws.

Dowel joints are stronger than butt or rabbet joints and they give a decorative effect. Drill matching holes in the corners to be joined. Use a peg or wood dowel the same diameter or slightly smaller than the hole you drilled and long enough to go into the holes in both pieces of wood. Use glue in the holes, push the dowel into one side of the wood, and line up with the other corner. If the dowels extend to the outer edge they will be decorative. Doweling can also be used on butt joints.

Miter and spline   **Rabbet**   **Tongue in groove**

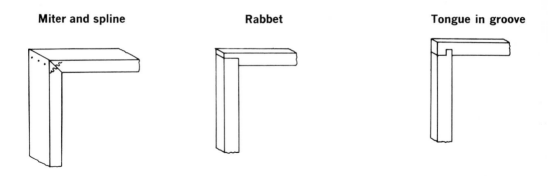

Miter. Each member is cut to an exact 45 degree angle (you can use a miter box or work carefully with a protractor or triangle); when assembled, they create a perfect 90 degree corner. A miter joint, like a butt joint, should be fastened with dowels or a spline or other reinforcing hardware. This joint is frequently used for frames.

The *rabbet* joint is a great improvement over the butt joint because one of the members is supported on two sides instead of only one. The rabbet joint must still be fastened by gluing and with screws or nails.

Tongue in groove consists of a grooved section in one board and a matching raised portion in the other board. It is a strong joint for corners and for shelves and compartments.

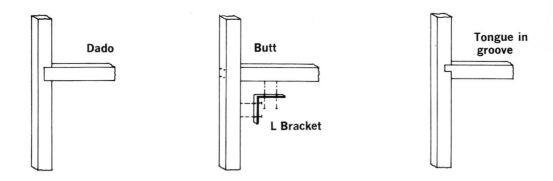

For shelves and to set in compartments, butt a strip of wood against the upright member and nail in or support with L brackets or other shelving devices available at a hardware store. You can also use doweling, a rabbet, or a tongue in groove joint.

MAKING THE PLASTIC BOX

Plastic is advantageously used for a box and for a covering for assembled environments. Plastic boxes may be purchased ready-made in a variety of sizes and thicknesses from display companies, photography suppliers, and florists where they are often sold for terrariums. Plastic containers in shapes other than the box may be adapted to specific imagery. Plastic is actually acrylic sheet sold under different brand names: Plexiglas, Lucite, and so on.

Ready-made boxes, and those you assemble yourself, will have bonded seams that give the appearance of multiplying or fragmenting

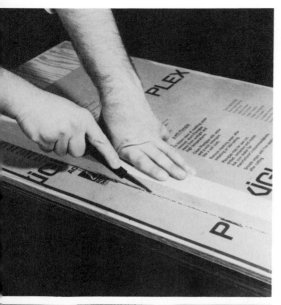

Acrylic sheet up to ¼ inch thick may be scribed and broken. Place the point of the special cutting tool at the edge of the cutting guide. Apply firm pressure and draw the cutting point the full width of the material.

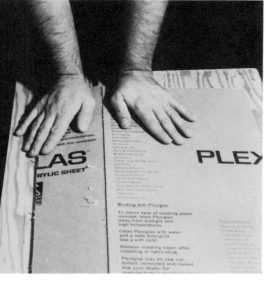

Position the scribed line face up over a wood dowel or rounded edge the same length as the plastic. Hold the sheet with one hand and apply downward pressure on the short side of the break with the other. Keep your hands adjacent to one another on each side of the line. Move down the line and break in successive positions along the scribed line. Don't try to scribe and break a portion less than about 1½ inches wide.

an object within and this effect can be used advantageously. You can also buy boxes without bonded seams; these are "extruded" or poured in a mold so that the plastic is all in one piece.

Making a plastic box depends on carefully measuring and squaring all the edges and corners to be bonded. Plastic sheet is sold in varying thicknesses such as ⅛ inch, ¼ inch, etc., in clear, colored, and a new mirror finish. It is also available in rods and tubes. An acetone or plastic solvent is required for bonding or joining. Glues used for glass, wood, or other materials will not work. You will need a saw or cutting tool, tape, and rulers.

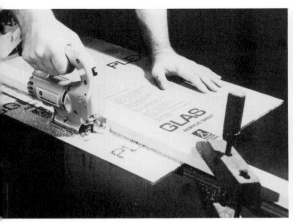

Acrylic sheet can be cut with any electric or hand saw. It is easier to cut if you leave the paper on. Peel paper off just before finishing to avoid scratching and fingerprinting. Use saw blades with 10 to 14 teeth per inch.

For neat joints, edges should be sanded before glueing and assembling. Use sandpaper on a block or use a fine file.

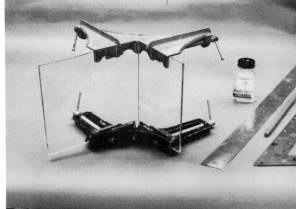

Apply the plastic solvent to both edges; solvent softens the molecular makeup of the plastic and allows the molecules to bind with one another. When dry, the edges harden together and the joint is clear. Apply solvent with a small brush, cotton tip, or a hypo-type needle available from plastic suppliers.

Edges can be clamped with a miter clamp or by placing pieces of masking tape across the joint.

CREATING SPECIAL EFFECTS

Throughout the book, you'll observe special effects achieved with magnifying lenses, mirrors, double images, and so forth. Finding concrete objects and methods to create these sequences requires imagination and ingenuity. The following methods are offered to familiarize you with materials and approaches you may not have thought of. You'll have to develop additional ones of your own.

Surrealistic and optical illusions can be accomplished by setting a lens in a plastic pane and mounting that pane within the box. The result is that one small portion of the object behind the lens will be enlarged; the lens will appear to hang in space because it is set into the clear plastic sheet.

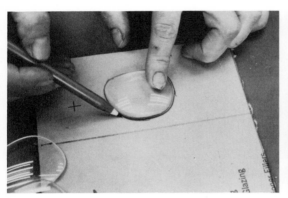 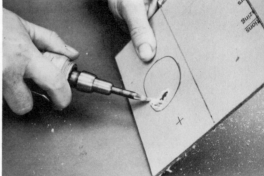

Outline the lens on the plastic.

Use a drill or other tool to cut a hole the same size as the lens.

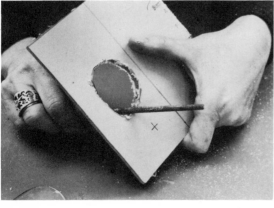 

Smooth the edges first with a file and then sandpaper.

When placed in front of a print, the lens will give a strange, but interesting, effect.

The bottoms of bottles often have magnifying or diminishing properties. You can use bottle bottoms over prints, glue the bottle to the inner side of the glass used for framing and set objects under them; the possibilities are infinite. Use a bottle cutter or a glass cutting hacksaw blade to cut the bottle.

Place the print, or other object, beneath for an illusion.

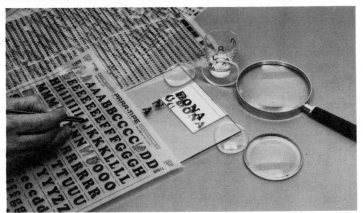

Alphabets and numerals are used in many of the boxes. If you cut letters out of paper and paste them on, they are opaque and the paper on which the letter is printed may ruin the effect you want. Instead use rub-on instant letters sold by art supply stores for use by advertising and graphic artists. Use a pen point to rub them off onto any kind of surface. When used on plastic or glass, you can create an effect of multiple letters. They are sold under trade names such as Letraset or Para-Tipe in a variety of size and type styles.

>

ALBERT'S SISTER. (Detail.) Joan Hall. The partially cut glass circle gives the illusion of a lens set into the outer glass frame. This heightens the interest over the face that is glued onto the back portion of the box. Pieces of mirror are set into the bottom and sides of the frame to reflect the portrait and to increase the illusion of depth in this portion of the box.

Courtesy, artist

TANGLEWOOD SKETCH BOX. Mary Bauermeister. 1972. Lenses with various degrees of magnification are set into the two layers of glass to achieve a variety of illusions and changing imagery of the assembled and drawn parts beneath. As the viewer changes his position, the curvatures of the various lenses alter the appearance of the shapes and images beneath. Notice the rabbetted joints of the box corners.

Courtesy, Galeria Bonino, Ltd., New York

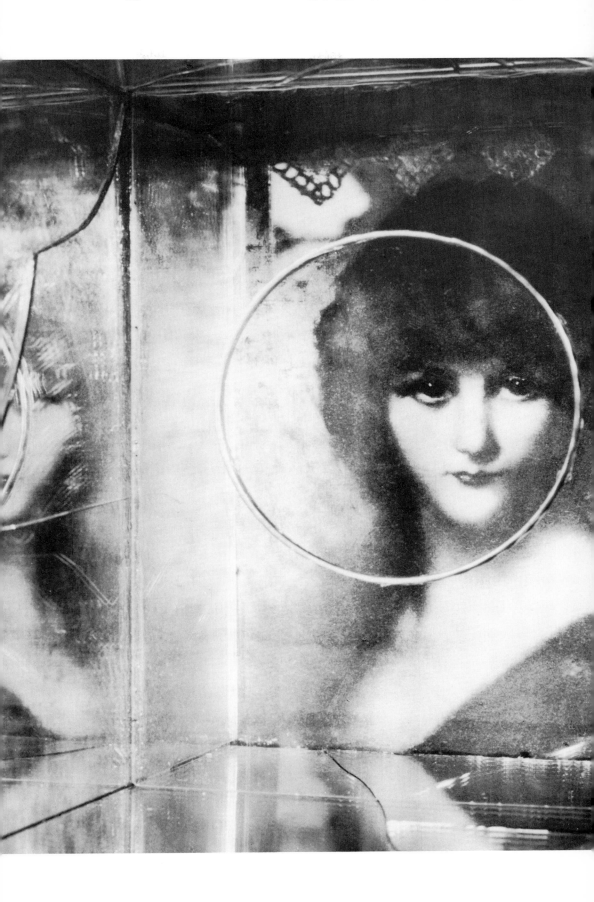

Assembled Materials

A MAJORITY OF SMALL BOX ENVIRONMENTS RELY HEAVILY ON an assemblage of found objects arranged in unexpected, new relationships to one another to present a message. The message may be very obvious or it may be obscure and symbolic. When no seemingly "meaningful" message exists, the artist may have arranged the items so that the viewer can bring his own set of perceptions to the scene and interpret it according to his personal faculties and experiences.

The creation of the assemblage within a box can begin from several artistic stimuli; perhaps an interesting box will suggest the setting for the microcosmic environment. An object may set off a series of visual and mental images and the artist will hunt for related objects. Perhaps he will have garnered the objects and then searched for a suitable box.

The assemblage box is open season for every conceivable imagery. Joan Hall and Art Schwerin use nostalgic themes. Geraldine Gladstone's boxes reflect her absorption in Oriental cultures. She purposely hunts for ancient artifacts, restores and uses them in a series of precious boxes that both contain and are objects of art. Claudia Chapline uses an old drawer as the environment for images made of fibers. Howard Woody's small box environments are often a vehicle for protesting the effects of pollution on the total environment. Phyllis Freeman's most delicious finds are old glove and other display cases into which she can suspend lenses, crystals, and other transparent objects that produce a variety of fantastic illusions.

In addition to the arrangements of the objects themselves, any and every other artistic medium and technique may be employed. Combine assemblage with printmaking, drawing, collage, decoupage, and any of the fiber techniques. Some artists concentrate the imagery only in the "contained" portion of the box; others consider the exterior as important a part of the overall canvas as the interior.

Technically, the only problems are those of adhering the materials to one another by carpentry methods or glueing. The range of available glues should be investigated. The Glue Chart on page 94 will help you select the proper glue for the materials to be adhered.

◄

NEST ANGEL. Joan Hall. 1973. 14½ inches high, 9 inches wide, 5¾ inches deep. Weathered wood box with another box inside. Bird nest, eggshell, glass, paper, and brass.

Courtesy, artist

COLLAGE—DECOUPAGE

Collage is the art of pasting papers onto a surface. It was first used by Pablo Picasso and Georges Braque in the early 1900s when they applied a portion of real paper to an oil-painted canvas.

The artist's studio often becomes an environment for his particular type of work. Jill Littlewood's studio has compartments and boxlike cubbyholes that mirror her interest in the box as a creative, expressive art form.

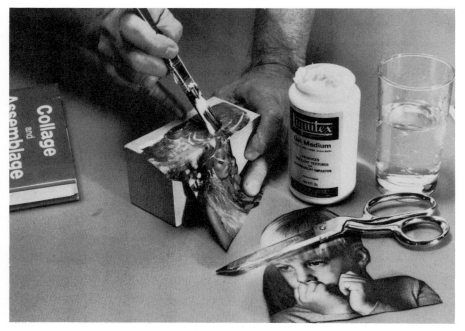

Collage techniques are a reliable adjunct to the assembled box. An infinite variety of images can be presented with pasted papers culled from magazines, posters, books, and other sources. For a super-realistic, slick, highly finished wedding of print to box, use the decoupage method of embedding a fine print beneath multiple coats of varnish.

Decoupage is also the art of applying a cut-out print to a surface, but in decoupage the print is completely embedded beneath multiple coats of varnish so that it appears to have been hand-painted. It was originally used on furniture and, though examples exist from early Chinese times, it was most popular in seventeenth-century Italy when it was dubbed a "poor man's art" because only the wealthy could afford the real hand painting.

Collage was developed as an "expressive" art while the decoupage heritage is considered a "decorative" art. Collage suggests an immediate impact between artist and viewer, and the image could be cut from a magazine, newsprint, posters, discarded papers, and the like. Decoupage suggests a slick, thoroughly planned application and the print is more likely a handsome, fine print made for the purpose. The box maker can adapt both techniques depending upon the presentation he wishes to achieve.

The collage cutout can be adhered to an object or to the inside or outside surface of the box with glue or with a polymer medium that will adhere and protect the surface. For decoupage, you need the fine print which must be sealed with a paper sealer before the varnish coats are applied. The print and box are usually coated with twenty to thirty layers of varnish which must be carefully sanded between each coat to eliminate bubbles and brush marks.

Other products available in art and craft supply stores can yield a variety of interesting effects. For example, a good reproduction of the Mona Lisa could be instantly altered with an antique or crackle finish. You can singe edges of a picture with a match or cigarette flame, or yellow the paper with bleach.

Every artist develops his own method of working; he gravitates toward the materials that hold the most appeal for him. California artist John Schroeder creates his box environments with organic pieces of the natural environment. He combs the desert for dried tree parts, bones, and weeds. A day's finds are spread out to dry; at the back, an arrangement is begun within a box.

He may develop two or more assemblages simultaneously, going from one to another, arranging and rearranging until he is pleased with the relationships of the pieces.

Mr. Schroeder makes his own frames using wood slats that he has mitered and clamped. These become the "front" for handmade boxes with depth. Glass is placed in the frame. Observe the frame clamps used for holding the mitered corners together until the glue hardens.

THE PLEDGE. John Schroeder. 1971. 12 inches high, 17½ inches wide, 4½ inches deep. Feathers, bottle, seed pods, plastic hands, beads, wood, glass, and dyes.

EVEN THE SMALLEST CRY IS HEARD. John Schroeder. 1973. 12 inches high, 15 inches wide, 7 inches deep. Bottles, feathers, colored sand, bird, wood, fabric. Frame with glass on both sides of the box.

Courtesy, artist

POLYESTER RESIN

Polyester resin is a liquid plastic that can have the appearance of glass or the opaqueness of marble. It can be used to embed diverse or similar objects in a thick medium, to duplicate objects by mold-making methods, or to create new forms.

For clear pours, you need only two basic ingredients; the polyester resin and a catalyst, or hardener, plus your mold or container. There are several formulations of polyester resin but the clear casting resin sold by craft and art suppliers appears to be most widely used in the boxes exhibited throughout the book. It is almost as clear as water, but it can be altered by using drops of coloring, or by adding pigments for textured effects. After the polyester is formed, it has the same properties as acrylic sheet in that it can be cut, painted on, sanded, polished, and so forth.

Always use polyester resin in a well-ventilated room and not where food is prepared. It dries, or cures, best in 70 degree temperatures. Setting time depends on the amount of catalyst added and the room temperature. With a little experimentation, you'll quickly get the feel of the materials and how to adapt them to your needs.

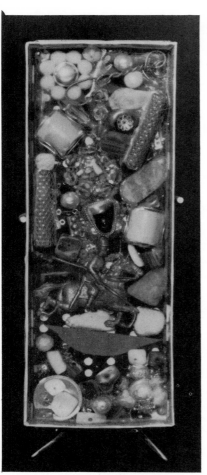

GRATE, GREAT. Louis Goodman. 1972. A discarded cheese grater becomes the container for objects embedded in polyester resin.

RAPUNZEL. Mary Bauermeister. 1965–66. 30-inch square. A box containing lens, glass pieces, stones, and collaged materials is set on a painted, assemblaged canvas. Objects are held within the box with clear polyester casting resin. Some of the objects are made of resin.
Courtesy, Galeria Bonino, Ltd.,
New York

Materials required are: polyester casting resin, catalyst (in small bottle—only about six drops are used to an ounce of resin), measuring cup, stirring sticks, and a mold. Objects to be embedded are optional. Plastic and paper molds are best as the resin shrinks from the mold without a separating medium. For metal and glass molds, rub the mold well with furniture wax or a coat of polyvinyl alcohol (PVA). When the resin is to become an intrinsic part of the box, do not use a release as it bonds permanently to the metal.

Follow specific product instructions for adding catalyst to resin. Thoroughly, but gently, stir for about one minute and pour resin into mold. Add objects for embedding, if desired. Objects may be added in the first pour, but if a thick transparent surface is desired, you can pour one layer, let cure, then place objects on that layer and add a second pour. The second layer could be colored, if desired.

Polyester resins can be made in any shape; the cup itself can become a mold. Newsprint, photos, and other images may be placed beneath the cured casting before it is assembled into the box. The foam packing piece, background, might also serve as a "container."

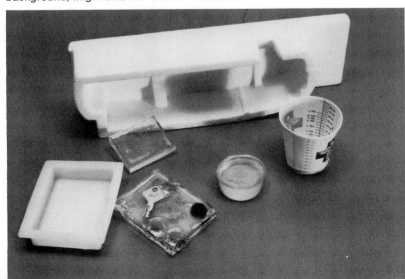

DESIGN CONSIDERATIONS

The box environment combines the problems of a two-dimensional surface and sculptural space so that several design considerations are involved. It is not sufficient to assemble assorted related objects and conclude that you have a "box environment." The elements of design and the presentation of a theme must be inherent.

Consider that the box has, first, interior and exterior surface. Second it has planes from front to back so that objects or prints might be placed on the back inner surface, in the center and at the

TEMPLE OF THE SIX SENSES. Geraldine Gladstone. 17 inches high, 16 inches wide, 9 inches deep. Gold leafed box with smaller boxes carefully arranged in the planes within. Bronze statues from India, Japan, and Thailand. The five senses are represented by the statues. Buddha represents the sixth sense. A gold fret extends the shape of the box at the top. The objects relate to suggest the theme. The design and coloring on the interior are carried to the exterior; both rely heavily on collaged prints.
Courtesy, artist

front of the box; some objects may protrude beyond the frontal plane. Third, there is the space from top to bottom and side to side. All the space must be consciously organized and dealt with so that there are large areas of greater interest, smaller areas of less interest. Where will the greatest interest be? It doesn't have to be in the center; it can be off center in the same way the painter plans a two-dimensional canvas. Objects themselves, because they exist in three dimensions, must be placed to occupy three-dimensional space in a sculptural relationship.

LOVE BOX. Geraldine Gladstone. 1973. 33 inches high, 25 inches wide, 5 inches deep. The objects are collected things the artist liked and those given to her by people she loved.

TO JUDY. Mike Sayers. 10 inches high, 21 inches wide. A shoe is an interesting form with which to begin a design and a theme. In this environment, ruby slippers are combined with crocheted pieces, feathers, foil, magic marker drawings, found objects, and neon lighting.
Courtesy, artist

BUDDHIST SHRINE. Geraldine Gladstone. 1972. 26 inches high, 13 inches wide, 10 inches deep. A once dilapidated box-chest with double pairs of doors has been repaired to become the environment for a set of images and objects assembled by the artist. The ancient Japanese Buddha figure was restored and the symbols within, around, and outside the box are combined with collage and gold leaf.

Courtesy, artist

THE BRIDE. Fritzie Abadi. 1973. 14 inches high, 8 inches wide, 6 inches deep. Mirror lined boxes, cricket cage, painted rocks, fabrics.
Photo, Peter A. Juley & Son, New York

BANK BOX. Joan Hall. 1973. 12½ inches high, 7½ inches wide, 5½ inches deep. Wood, paper, pennies, Plexiglas.
Courtesy, artist

HORACE GREELEY. Geraldine Gladstone. 5 inches high, 3 inches wide, 1½ inches deep. This tiny box is like a jewel with its papered interior, picture of Horace Greeley, odd shaped hardened metal drippings and amber marble.
Courtesy, artist

EGG BOX NO. 1. John Henry. 18 inches high, 10 inches wide, 7 inches deep. Wood, leather, marble, slate, hay, feathers, eggs, spoon, button hook, tweezers, pin holder, ivory handled pic, plumb bob, egg cup, Plexiglas, brass hinges, and lock.
Courtesy, artist

BABAK. Claudia Chapline. 1973. 7½ inches high, 10 inches wide, 15 inches deep. Wood drawer lined with dyed feathers becomes a nesting place for three mohair forms shaped like river stones. These are bound into the box with pale blue mohair yarn.

Courtesy, artist

UNTITLED. John Schroeder. 1973. 4½ inches high, 29 inches wide, 21½ inches deep. (Plexiglas cover removed for photography.) Glass bottles, feathers, beads, sand, cactus.

DOCTEUR COLLODION'S CABINET OF CURIOSITIES. Arthur Schwerin. 1974. 19½ inches high, 24 inches wide, 6 inches deep. An assemblage of turn-of-the-century nostrums including strange potions and lotions, electrical mail-order "cure-alls," and curious remedies.

Photo, Garry

UNTITLED. Ellen Sherwood. 1973. 7 inches high, 5 inches wide, 3 inches deep. Glazed ceramics set in a ceramic box form.

Courtesy, artist

PANDORA'S BOX. Norma Minkowitz. 30 inches wide, 16 inches deep. Stitchery, crochet, plucking, and padding.

Courtesy, artist

LAMENT. (Einstein). Julian de Miskey. 1973. Papier-mâché over wire armatures. Newsprint, hand painting, music fragments. All symbolize the threatened destruction of science and art, the things most important to Einstein. A background scene of an atomic explosion is coupled with appeals in heavy newsprint to outlaw the H-bomb.

Courtesy, artist
Photo, Charles Anderson

OBJECTS. U.S.A. John Henry. 20 inches high, 20 inches wide, 9 inches deep. Woodcut, brass tacks, chromed egg, sterling silver hot dog, glass eye, mirrors, plastic objects, mannequin hand, flags, feathers, felt, assorted woven textiles, enamel, acrylic, mat board, leather strap.

Courtesy, artist

CARMEN MIRANDA. Sabato Fiorello. 1974. Lucite box with collage, color transparencies, and objects.

Courtesy, artist

CREATION. Arthur Schwerin. 1973. 19½ inches high, 12½ inches wide, 6 inches deep. Biblical metaphors are mingled with filament from a modern light bulb. A large magnifying glass emphasizes a Dürer print. A hermit crab emerges from a shell, fruit and a marble egg give a poetic meaning to the biblical phrase, *and there shall be light.*

Courtesy, artist

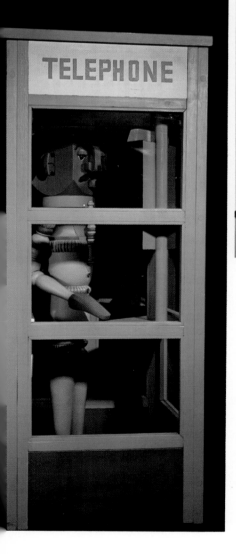

THE TELEPHONE BOOTH. Jacqueline Fogel. 1973. 36 inches high. Handmade figure and booth reconstructed from discarded wood objects.

Collection, Gloria and Bernard Mindich,
New York
Photo, Rupert Finegold

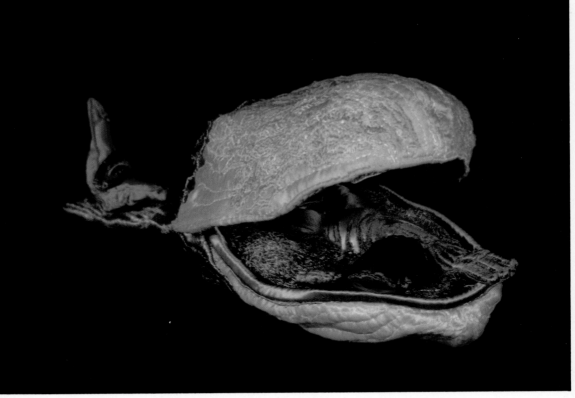

THE MELON, THE FROG, AND THE SNAIL.   Deborah Frederick. 1974. Fabrics and fibers, quilted, stuffed, and embroidered.
Courtesy, artist

LAGUNA BEACH ABALONE.   Stephen Blumrich. 1974. 5 inches high, 5 inches wide, 4 inches deep. Stuffed batik fabric with seashell.
Courtesy, artist

Above

FUR LADY. Tom Duncan. 1973. 24 inches high. Two cigar boxes, vacuum formed plastic, collage, and acrylic.

Courtesy, artist

Above right

THE GREEN MADONNA AND HER FRIENDS. (Detail.) Tom Duncan. 1974. 6½ feet high. Wood, collage, plaster, fur, acrylic set in an old box from an amusement arcade.

Courtesy, artist

Right

WINDOWBOX. Judith Citrin. 1973. 7½ inches high, 11 inches wide, 7 inches deep. Wood box with glass, mirror, ceramics, paper collage, and satin.

AMPHIBIEN '83. Alice Balterman. 1972. 10 inches high, 14 inches wide, 3 inches deep. Found wood, stamp, framed photo, shells, graduate glass, printing plate, old photo, wood ball, beads, and old book cover in a shadow box.
Courtesy, artist

THEATRE OF THE UPSIDE DOWN. Gordon Wagner. 1974. 21 inches high, 21 inches wide, 4½ inches deep. A mirrored bottom reflects a sky drawn on the underside of the floor-board. A ship and water painted on the rock becomes the stage for the tiny figure. The gate is made of wood dowels painted black; the back of the box is drawn to suggest deep perspective. At the top, a city is drawn upside down.

THREE MUSES. Edward K. Higgins. 1973. Closed: 6 inches high, 2½ inches wide, 2½ inches deep. Open: 6 inches high, 6¾ inches wide. Sterling silver, lost wax centrifugal cast and assembled.

Photo, artist

FUN ARCADE. Arthur Schwerin. 1973. 25 inches high, 16½ inches wide, 6 inches deep. A sentimental journey to an amusement park. A fluorescent carnival backdrop sets the stage for a fun house mirror, oversize ice cream cone, and objects out of scale to suggest the way a child looks at things. A flickering electric light is mounted behind the title card to heighten the illusion of the tableau.

Courtesy, artist

CITYSCAPE. Alice Balterman. 1970. 16 inches high, 32 inches wide, 2 inches deep. Found wood objects and scraps, magazine photos, and paint in a type font drawer.
Collection, Mr. & Mrs. A. S. Braude, Cincinnati, Ohio Photo, artist

SUMMER '72. (Detail.) Jill Littlewood. 1972. Shells and related found objects arranged in a type font drawer.
Courtesy, artist

V.F.W. CONVENTION. Phyllis Freeman. 8 inches high, 12 inches wide, 6 inches deep. Plastic, cloth, paper, mirror, emblems, acrylic paint.

FIRST AID. (Two views.) Ben Talbert. 1965. 13 inches high, 13 inches wide, 5¾ inches deep.

Courtesy, artist

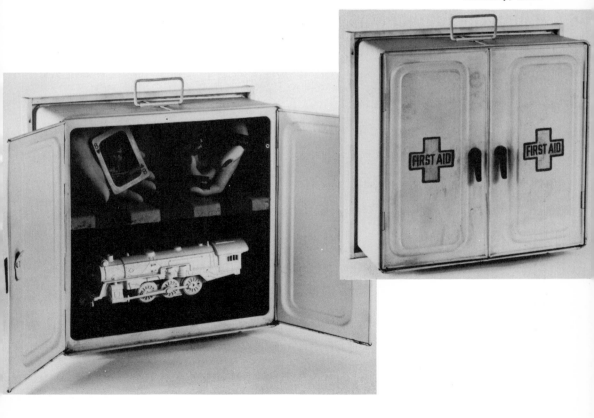

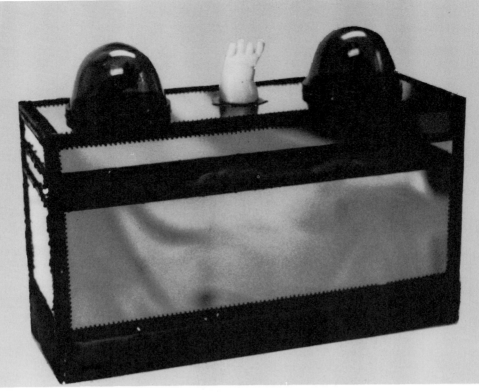

POLLUTION. Howard Woody. 1970. 14 inches high, 18 inches wide, 7 inches deep. The box assumes the role of a coffin. An inserted glass strip opens the view to an interior mirrored area containing three doll heads buried in sand. Three grasping hands appear to protrude through the top; two are covered with blue domes.

Courtesy, artist

TEXAS COWBOY RIDING A JACKRABBIT. Craig Kauffman. 1973. 4 inches high, 6 inches wide, 2½ inches deep. Rope, barbed wire, sand, glass, cork, beads, fish in formaldehyde, postcard.

Courtesy, artist

BOXED BAGS. Susan H. Brown. 9 inches high, 12 inches wide. An old double box with doors holds bags with yellow and orange strings. Divisions in the box are covered with felt.

Courtesy, artist

704 HINSDALE STREET. Ray Friedberg. Box assemblage with additional boxes of varying depths set within.

Courtesy, artist

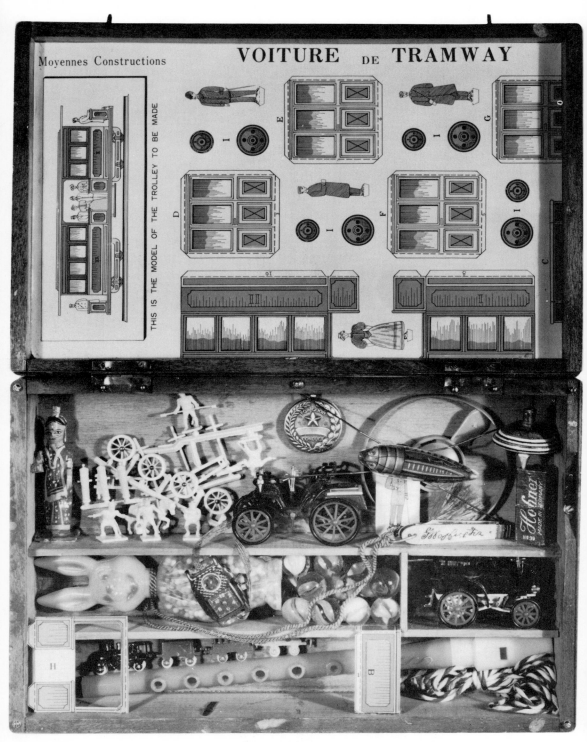

TROLLEY TO TOYLAND. Arthur Schwerin. 1973. French tramway cutout card for children. Toys set in the top of a lidded box. Toys are assembled in the bottom compartments.

Courtesy, artist

BACK WOODS TOWN. Alice Balterman. 1972. 8 inches high, 13 inches wide, 5 inches deep. Magazine photos, found wood, and twigs with drawing in an old box.

BEWARE OF BEAR. Alice Balterman. 1973. 7½ inches high, 20 inches wide, 2 inches deep. Italian game, perspective prints, printing blocks and type, toy, small box fragments, all set in a crate cart.

KEYS & CO. Alice Balterman. 1971. 5 inches high, 10 inches wide, 1 inch deep. Old keys, mirrors, type blocks, watch gears, set in an old compartmented drawer.

Photos, Jeff Darby

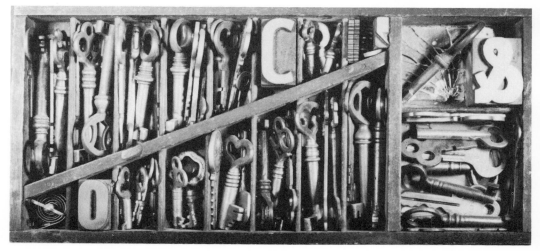

FOLK-SORRY.   Raymond Barnhart.   30 inches high, 18 inches wide, 6 inches deep.   A
fabric lined box with a fragmented musical instrument has a surreal-cubist effect.

Courtesy, artist

ARMY OF 50 CLOWNS. Cyril Miles. 1965. ¾ inches deep. Printer's font
drawer is loaded with objects that represent Americana junk stuff within and
on top of the compartments. It is nostalgia emptied out of pockets, bags,
and drawers. Sugar loaves, candy wrapper—the world of penny candy days
gone by.

Photo, Milstein

MORNING OF THE LAST DAY. Sandra Jackman. 12 inches high, 12 inches wide, 4 inches deep.
Courtesy, artist

CARDINAL'S COVENANT. Tom Duncan. 5½ feet high.
Courtesy, artist

SECRET HIDING PLACE. Sandra Jackman. 11 inches high, 8½ inches wide, 8 inches deep.
Courtesy, artist

REFLECTION. Phyllis Freeman.
1968. 18 inches high, 16 inches
wide, 9 inches deep. Old display box, lenses, and mirrors.

TEARS. Phyllis Freeman. 1968.
25½ inches high, 12½ inches
wide, 7 inches deep. Chandelier
tear-drop prisms, old glove display box, peacock feather.
Collection, George Schneider,
Chicago

STUDIO AT DORKING.   Gordon Wagner.   1973.   18 inches high, 15 inches wide, 6 inches deep.
All parts except the toy cannon are handmade.

Constructions

MANY BOX MAKERS PREFER TO CONSTRUCT THE IMAGES THEY use in their boxes rather than assemble found objects. This enables them to achieve exactly the effects they want and to exercise complete control of the materials, colors, textures, and sizes. The artist is like the stage designer, creating an entire background for the scene he sets within the box.

The box itself may or may not be handmade; but most likely the majority of objects within are constructed by the artist. Clay is used extensively because of its versatility. One can model and mold with clay, use bisque or glaze finishes, create whole images, portions of images, and fragments. By making a plaster mold you can duplicate objects exactly. Fritzie Abadi creates assorted ceramic shapes to use for heads and other body parts in her boxes.

Julian de Miskey's themes present a social satire using the box in the tradition that Bosch, Goya, and Hogarth used paint and drawing. He creates the box of wood or Lucite. The figures are mostly papier-mâché molded over wire armatures. These are combined with collage, handmade scenery, and some found objects.

Soft items within a box may be created with foam rubber, by sewing and stuffing a form, by crochet, knitting, or other fiber techniques. Fabrics and fibers are used extensively in the examples by Gwynne Lott and Colette. Lucas Samaras sometimes creates the entire box and its contents from soft materials.

The constructed box may contain many illusions: foils and mirrors that reflect, wood blocks that are nearly flat but are drawn upon to suggest perspective, suspended shapes that appear to float in space as though called back from another world by some occult medium. Surrealism is achieved by an unrealistic sense of scale between objects and settings.

47

· THE CASTLE OF THE GRAF VAN RHOMELGHEM, right, by Gordon Wagner illustrates the involvement required to construct a box environment. Mr. Wagner's boxes often have moving parts that are planned to fool the eye, to take you beyond the realm of the ordinary projection of the imagination. They are like mini-dramas on a mini-stage. All parts are meticulously calibrated and engineered as though the box was a life-size stage with moveable props for real actors and actresses.

   Mr. Wagner's working drawing, below, illustrates the planning necessary. Almost all parts are created by hand. Metal liner and ball bearings are used. The box itself is hand-constructed; the platform beneath the figures contains the mechanism. The checkerboard floor is hand-painted, the figures are modeled of self-hardening clays. Walls and other props are made of Fome-Cor, lightweight wood, or heavyweight cardboard. Mirrors are used extensively.

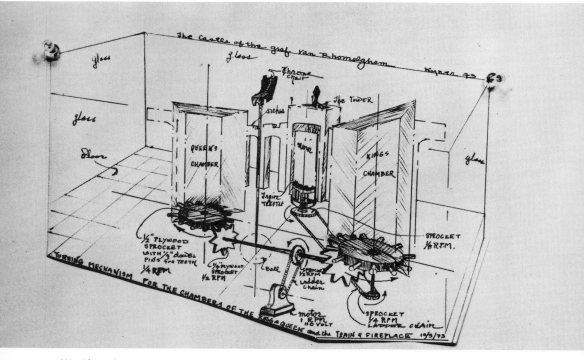

Working drawing showing the mechanisms and plan for THE CASTLE OF THE GRAF VAN RHOMELGHEM. Gears are arranged beneath the box so that the chambers of the king and queen rotate as does the guard's chamber.

THE CASTLE OF THE GRAF VAN RHOMELGHEM. Gordon Wagner. 1973. 22 inches high, 3 inches wide, 20 inches deep. Front view: The facade of the castle is closed and the guard waits quietly in his box.

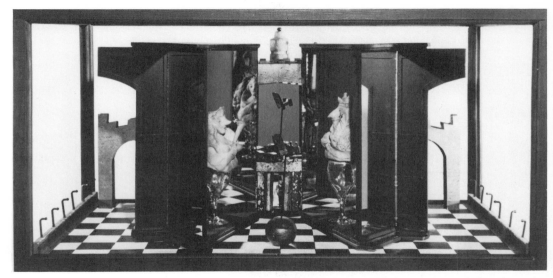

Open view: As the sections turn mechanically, the king and queen appear in their mirrored boxes perched on glass goblet thrones.

Rear of the castle with towers and gates.

Courtesy, artist

The basic box and the individual parts have been constructed. Receptacles have been planned in the floor to accept the movable parts; the motorized units are in the base of the box.

A portion is placed on the box; it is one of the movable parts that turns along with the king's and queen's chambers.

A metal cylinder accepts the wood shaft. It will be held to the floor by the gear mechanism; see next photo.

Portion of gears at bottom of box. Note how the floor has additional supports of wood strips that also hold the metal cylinders.

The king is carved of clay and will be brightly painted with acrylics.

The chamber is hand-built and lined with mirrors.

The completed box is enclosed with glass and the framing strips attached.

Demonstration, Gordon Wagner

THE BLACK WIDOW IN SEARCH OF A MATE. Fritzie Abadi. 18 inches high, 9 inches wide, 6 inches deep. Mirror-lined boxes with handmade cut-out and painted shapes.

Photo, Peter A. Juley & Son

BY THE SEA SIDE. Fritzie Abadi. 16 inches high, 6 inches wide, 4 inches deep. Handmade and natural objects are combined.

Photo, Peter A. Juley & Son

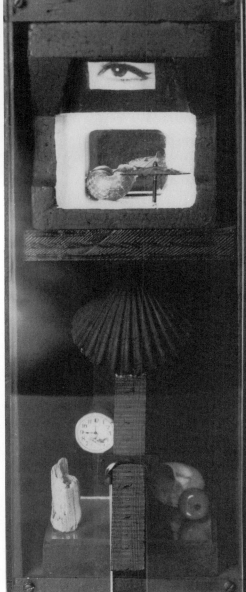

(opposite, above)
THE QUEEN'S BEDROOM. Gordon Wagner. 1973. 22 inches high, 18 inches wide, 4 inches deep. All handmade pieces result in a miniature dresser set in a box. Playing card and lace.

Photo, Jim Goss

◄

DEVIL'S TRIANGLE. Gordon Wagner. 1973. 19 inches high, 19 inches wide, 5½ inches deep. A ship sails on a square world. It is shown falling again and again in the perils of the deep. The background is tones of dark blues and purples and it is curved to oppose the square "globe."

ENVIRONMENT FOR A WINGED BEING. Irene Salava. 1973. 14 inches high, 8 inches wide, 7 inches deep. Handmade box on wheels with metal drippings and shapes. A winged being (below) nestles in the leather- and fur-lined cavity. The cover is also lined with leather. The being is made of wood, has movable joints, and a bejeweled face with fur hair.

BEEBLES. Gwynne Lott. 1973. Graduated size boxes are lined with stuffed soft fabric. The bottom box houses the mother, the center box, the father, and the top box, the children. Parents are made of leather with fur painted features. Children are fabrics.

JUDITH CITRIN'S UNIQUE BOXES BEGIN WITH A SLIDING LID cigar box. Other items are a combination of handmade and found objects. Says Ms. Citrin: "The box is my vehicle of expression; it 'contains.' It is a vessel for the dream, the secret, the elusive, unconscious image. My work corresponds to life's two realities. The outer, public self we present to the world, and the inner . . . without mask, and filled with the tumble of brief images that fill our dreams, fantasies and sometimes linger on in memory. The imagery comes from my unconscious and hopefully will speak to those feelings of the viewer, rather than convey a literal meaning."

The basic box is a cigar box with a sliding lid. It is decorated and embellished by hand painting with acrylics and with collage.

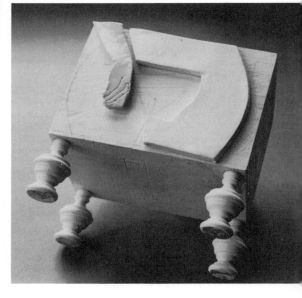

The box is covered with a coat of gesso and marked for placement of objects. The feet are made from wood turnings; either old knobs or ready-made pieces purchased from a lumber or do-it-yourself shop. The hand and raised torso shape are made from glazed fired clay.

To create the breast forms from glazed ceramics, a mold was made using the top of the egg form from L'eggs hosiery. Notice that the mold was made in a plastic cottage cheese container. The glazed breasts are placed on the lid of the box.

MILLIE BOX III. Judith Citrin. 1974. 7½ inches high, 7 inches wide, 5 inches deep. The completed box with painting and photograph collaged onto the box.

The interior of the box has been fitted with a mirror that reflects the photo pasted on the under side of the lid.

BIG TITZ II. Judith Citrin. 1973. 5 inches high, 7 inches wide, 7 inches deep. Hinged cigar box becomes the environment for stuffed cotton shapes that are reflected in a mirror on the under side of the lid. Breasts are made of plastic shapes. Hand painting and collage.

HER VERY SPECIAL GOODIE BOX. Judith Citrin. 1973. 11 inches high, 7 inches wide, 7½ inches deep. Wood, mirror, plaster, hair, and hand painting.

WINDOWBOX. Judith Citrin. 7½ inches high, 11 inches wide, 7 inches deep. Wood, glass, mirror, ceramic, paper collage, satin.

CORN ON THE COB. (Two views.) Judith Citrin. 1973. 13½ inches high, 4½ inches wide, 12 inches diameter. Wood, velvet, aluminum, plaster, plastic hand painting, and collage.

ELEPHANT TRUNK. Linda Kramer. 1973. 11 inches high, 31 inches wide, 10 inches deep. Glazed ceramic forms set in fur.

CHANGE. Linda Kramer. 1974. 12 inches high, 18 inches wide, 12 inches deep. Highly textured yellow glazed ceramic shapes with unplied rope.

HORNY. Linda Kramer. 1974. 15 inches diameter, 8 inches high. Ceramic shapes project from a round cake box.

FAREWELL TO SPARTA. Fritzie Abadi. 19 inches high, 16 inches wide, 10 inches deep. Cricket cages contain ceramic figures made by the artist, painted cloth faces, and other objects.

Photo, Peter A. Juley & Son

THE WORLD FAMOUS LIME BROTHERS. Robert Middaugh. 1973. 8 inches high, 10 inches wide, 3 inches deep. Fiberboard handmade box with cutaway circles to reveal three ceramic faces.

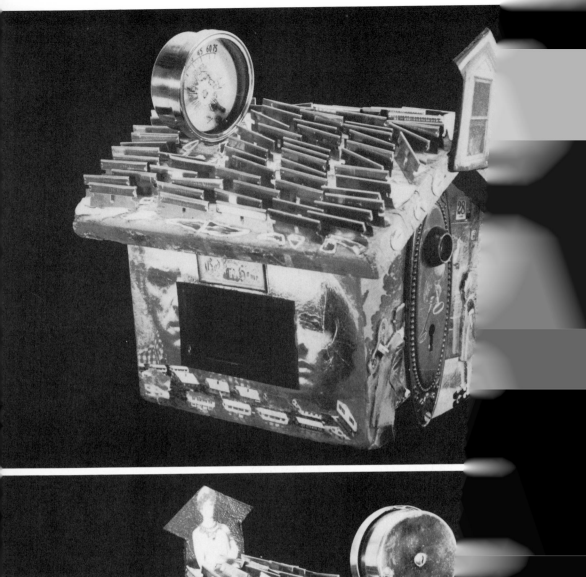

THE GAME BOX. Phyllis Freeman. 1969. 38 inches high, 18 inches wide, 6 inches deep. Collage, painted parts, plastic, drawing, and lettering.
Collection, Dr. & Mrs. Mel Meilach, Chicago

◄

CONDEMNED TO MEANING. (Two views.) Phyllis Freeman. 1973. 11 inches high, 9 inches wide, 9½ inches deep. Wood birdhouse, razor blades, paper collage, cardboard, mirror, objects, acrylic paint.

DREAMING TRUE. Michael McNeill. 1973. Constructed wood box of bird's-eye maple, lace, fur, bird's head.
Courtesy, artist

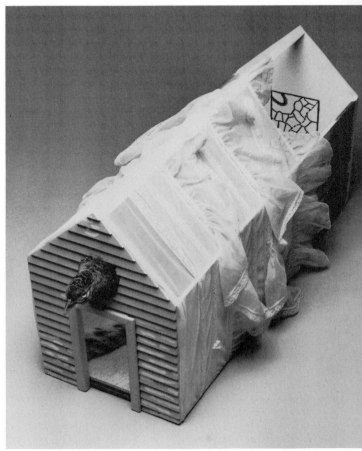

JAIL HOUSE BLUES or OH IF WE COULD ONLY HANG OUR CLOTHES ON THE LINE. Fritzie Abadi. 1974. 10 inches high, 15 inches wide, 12 inches deep. Wood boxes, mirrors, painted ceramic faces, cut-out cloth clothes.

Photo, Peter A. Juley & Son

THE BULL. Fritzie Abadi. 1972. Wood, mirrors, photos, collage, and ceramics.

Photo, Peter A. Juley & Son

THE RENAISSANCE. Julian de Miskey.
1974. 30 inches high, 27 inches wide,
10 inches deep. A Fra Angelico print
dominates the painted background; a
painted hanged man is at left. Figures
are papier-mâché over wire armatures;
the table is wood and the goblets are
plastic bottle caps.

Photo, Charles Anderson

PROMETHEUS. Julian de Miskey. 1974.
30 inches high, 22 inches wide, 9 inches
deep. Shaped cardboard covered with
gesso forms the background for the
papier-mâché figure attached with chains.
The vulture is papier-mâché and feathers
over wire. Some collage and painting.

Photo, Charles Anderson

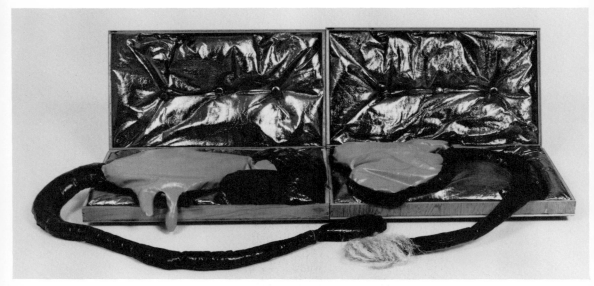

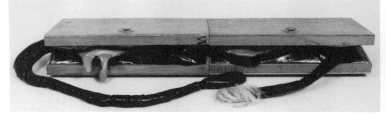

DOUBLE COW CASE. (Open view above, closed view below.) Barbara Kirchhoff. Two horizontally attached boxes contain soft sculptured cows. One is a bull, the other a cow complete with zipper vagina. The background material is copper colored aluminum foil fabric.

COW CASE. Barbara Kirchhoff. A composite cow, represented by yellow, red, and black vinyl, is neatly fitted in a lined plywood case. The hard shell box separates the soft environment from the world outside. The artist feels that "they are womb-like; soft, delicate and private; fragile in their own way."

FIT FOR A KING . . . OR EVEN A QUEEN. (Open and closed views.) Barbara Kirchhoff. 1973. 20-inch cube. The cube opens diagonally to reveal a rich interior of black vinyl with a pillow form of colored aluminum foil fabric and covered buttons.

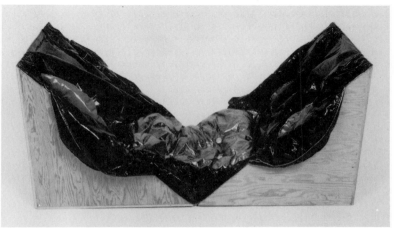

EGGBERRY BOX. Barbara Kirchhoff. Small, hand crocheted egg-berries rest on excelsior.

All photos, Charles Cox

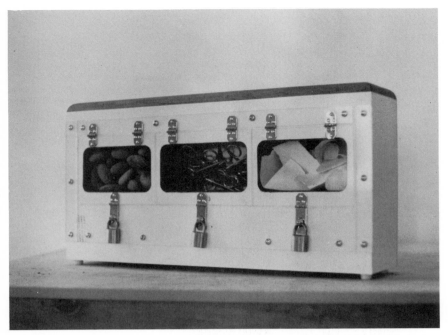

ROCKS, SCISSORS, PAPER. William C. Tunberg. 12 inches high, 24 inches wide, 6 inches deep. The cabinet is handmade and contains the kinds of objects that the artist feels people are obsessed with and the orders that they impose on their lives.

Courtesy, artist

WIDOW IN A BOX. Elsie Shaw. 1962. 16 inches high, 16 inches wide, 7 inches deep. Plywood box and setting, welded copper figure, dog and frame, fabric, collage, and wallpaper.

Courtesy, artist

ENVIRONMENT AND PERFORMANCE.
Colette. 1973.

TRANSFORMATION OF THE SLEEP-
ING GYPSY. Colette. 1973. Para-
chute nylon is arranged in both
boxes with handmade doll figures.
Courtesy, Stefanotty Gallery,
New York

ERROL FLYNN ICON. Sabato Fiorello. 1973. 15 inches high, 8 inches
wide, 4½ inches deep. Photographs, 3M ''Color-in-Color'' transparencies,
and color photocopies, found objects, plastic boxes, and dividers.
Photographed at Orlando Gallery, Encino, California

Plastics

VARIOUS PLASTIC MATERIALS HAVE BEEN INGENIOUSLY adapted to the box environment. The plastic box itself suggests a modern, slick, uncluttered statement that is deftly combined with contemporary techniques by Sabato Fiorello, Ted Metz, and Antoni Miralda. Plastic foam figures and settings are sculptured by Indiana artist Arlene Seitzinger. Other examples explore plastics as an artistic medium. Plastics can be made to serve the creative needs of the contemporary artist very well, providing a counter-argument to those who condemn "our plastic society."

Sabato Fiorello prefers two kinds of plastic boxes: the icon shape with doors which he has fabricated by a plastics company; the second type is the wide assortment that he culls from every packaging manufacturer possible—plastic boxes used for jewelry, medicines, notions, and whatever. These are used within the larger icon boxes or in separate statements.

But Fiorello has adapted another contemporary industrial technique to his artistic presentation. He relies heavily on the unique photocopy imagery available with a 3M "Color-in-Color" system. The machine is as easy to use as a photocopy machine available in an office or library. The difference is that this 3M system reproduces colors of the original; it can change the colors of the original print, separate colors, and reproduce the color print on a sheet of transparent film which may be adhered to the plastic box.

The machine is available at 3M color centers in major cities. Prints can be sent to the color centers for reproduction. If a local industry rents the machine an artist may be able to use the unit at off hours and reimburse the company for its paper. Consult a local 3M sales center for information about a machine near you.

Photocopies in black and white can easily be incorporated into box environments if the color units are not accessible. Fiorello's use of duplicate images in his icon boxes can stimulate additional approaches to the creation of small box environments.

71

The 3M "Color-in-Color" system is a photocopy process that reproduces original color prints. A greater advantage is that it can alter the colors in a print, it can put color into a black and white image, it can produce color separations. With a special paper in the machine, one can get a matrix copy that allows the color to be transferred to a sheet of transparent acetate.

To make a transparency, the colored matrix copy is placed on a heat transfer unit with a sheet of acetate; the ink from the copy is transferred to the acetate. The acetate is available in different colors. Because copies can also be made in different colors and in color separations, the range of possible variations is infinite.

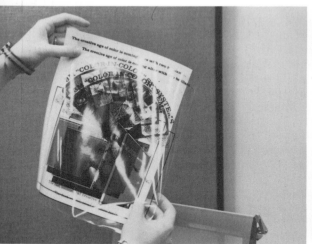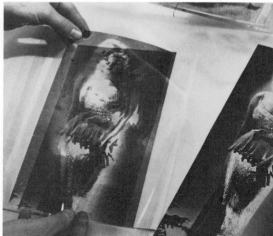

The copy and acetate with color transferred onto it are removed from the heat transfer unit.

When complete the artist has three images to work with: the original photo, the color copy (some of the ink still remains on the matrix after the transfer), and the acetate sheet. It is these multiple images that Sabato Fiorello incorporates into his icon boxes.

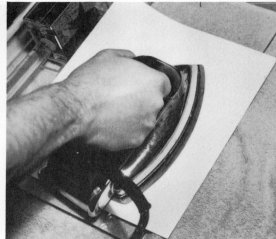

Sabato Fiorello uses essentially collage and assemblage methods combined with the 3M "Color-in-Color" system. The box is made from ½- to ¾-inch-thick clear or opaque Lucite. The front covers are hinged. He uses multiples of smaller plastic boxes, rods, cement, cutting instruments, found objects, and illustrations. Photos of movie stars are taken from high quality film history books. Sometimes he is able to buy old photos from movie studios or private collections.

The heat process used to transfer a matrix color copy to a transparent sheet of acetate is applied differently here. Instead of transferring the matrix copy to acetate, color is transferred directly to the Lucite door. Use an iron set at 280 degrees (between the cotton and linen settings). Put a protective piece of paper between print and iron and apply even pressure for about 15 minutes. Lift corner to determine how the print is transferring.

A transferred matrix copy and the original photograph. When transferring a print, you must be careful not to overheat or the Lucite may buckle and turn yellow.

One effect might be a double image; the color print on the top of the Lucite and the original beneath. You can also apply the acetate transparency directly to the Lucite by glueing with plastic cement; glue the top of the acetate that does not contain the color. If you apply glue to the color image, there is a tendency for it to spot.

The plastic boxes within the large box contain items that relate to the actor's life or to the particular role that is idolized in the box's content. This box will portray the symbols and objects that pertain to Clark Gable. Objects are placed in the box and the head of Gable is being cut out with an X-acto knife.

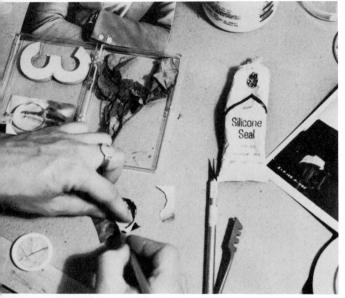

Paper is adhered to plastic with clear Silicone Seal.

An optical illusion may be created within the box by adhering a magnifying glass over one portion of the picture for distortion and emphasis.

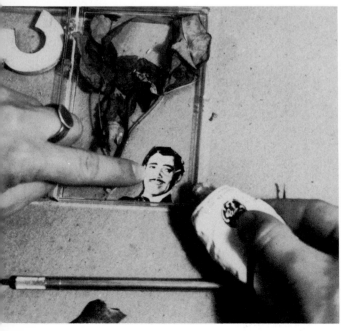

CLARK GABLE ICON BOX.
Sabato Fiorello. 1974. The
finished box with color trans-
fers on the outer doors and
the original photo on the inside back. Portions of the left-
over color matrix have been
cut up and used inside the
smaller boxes.

The closed box.
Collection, Phil Orlando,
Encino, California

75

THREE ENVIRONMENTS. Ted Metz.
1973. 16 inches high, 13 inches
wide, 10 inches deep. Acrylic
plastic, aluminum, carved acrylic,
sand, tree parts, Formica.
Courtesy, artist

HOLLYWOOD. Sabato Fiorello. 1974.
12 inches high, 12 inches wide, 4
inches deep. A series of boxes set
into a large box. Each box contains
images of different Hollywood stars.

MARILYN MONROE. Sabato Fiorello. 1970.
12 inches high, 12 inches wide, 4 inches
deep. Another concept of multiple boxes
within a large box. Each box cover contains a fragmented portion of the image.
The boxes are removable and can be in-
terchanged. Each box contains photos and
assembled parts.
*Photographed at Orlando Gallery,
Encino, California*

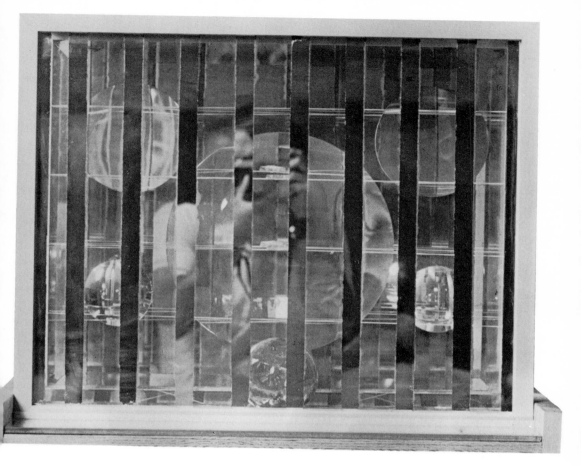

IMAGE BOX. Raymond Barnhart. 1972. 18 inches high, 20 inches wide, 5 inches deep. A sheet of plastic has been scored with circles and horizontal lines. It was cut into strips and mounted in the front portion of a box to alter and fragment the images within and on the back of the box.

Courtesy, artist

SOLDADES (Soldiers). Antoni Miralda. 1971. Assemblage of plastic soldiers in boxes. Each box presents a different color; each soldier is glued on individually with plastic cement.

Courtesy, Galerie Boutique Germain, Paris

Arlene Seitzinger has developed a sculptural technique for plastic foam images. Different thicknesses of foam are available from fabric shops where it is sold for upholstering purposes, pillows, bolsters, etc. It can be found in the Sears catalog; other sources are listed in the classified pages of the telephone book under "Plastics." The supplies are simple: a piece of foam; cutting tools are a hacksaw blade, carving knife, scissors, and tweezers; coloring materials; and pointed rods.

The shape is marked on the foam with the Magic Marker, then cut through using a hacksaw blade in your hand. Pull the foam apart as you cut.

 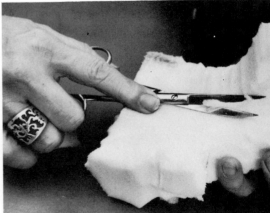

Continue rounding out the large shape with the blade.

Refine the shape and achieve texture with the small scissors. A curved cutting blade, such as a manicure scissors, helps yield necessary shapes.

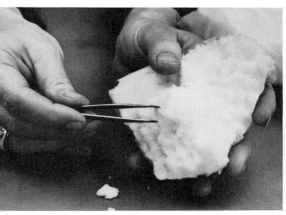

For the tree leaf texture, pieces of the foam are plucked away with an eyebrow tweezers.

Color can be applied with spray paints or with Magic Markers. Overall coloring for large pieces of foam can be done by dipping the foam into any household fabric dye, then letting the foam dry.

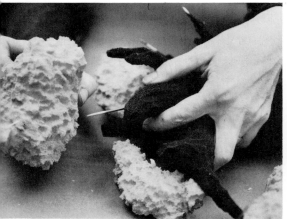

Pieces are assembled by poking them together over double pointed pieces of wire. Use lengths of coat hangers and grind them to a point on a grinding wheel.

The finished foam form is placed in a plastic box and adhered where necessary with silicone caulking material. For the watery environments of the figures (see next page), distilled water is used and the box is tightly sealed.

BALLERINAS. Arlene Seitzinger. 1973. The seam of the bottom box gives an illusion of many more than the actual six legs.

FRONT PORCH. (In progress.) Arlene Seitzinger. 1974. Walls and porch of foam over a wood form. All objects and figures are made of foam.

MONSTERS. (Three views.) Arlene Seitzinger. 1973. The straight-on view shows the one monster in the water environment.

Second view: The corner seam doubles the image and the sides reflect.

Third view: The top view again shows the illusion of more than one.

UNIVERSAL AND MGM. Phyllis Freeman. 1973. A one quart milk bottle contains sculptured plaster and Paris-craft (plaster impregnated tape).

Other Approaches to the Box Environment

EXAMPLES SO FAR HAVE CONCENTRATED ON THE BOX FORM as the container. Inevitably, the creative person breaks out of the box for some of his statements so that the box is supplanted by another container.

Following the exhibit in Illinois and Wisconsin titled SMALL ENVIRONMENTS which concentrated on box forms, a California gallery requested examples for a show to be titled ENVIRONMENTS IN A BOTTLE. This opened up another set of problems for the artist and the results were a far cry from the traditional sailor's pastime of building a ship inside a jar. Bottles could be interpreted to be any size, any shape. They could be large enough for the hands to work within or so tiny that not much more than a poured material could be placed within. Bottle cutters were used; the environments created within the glass bottles and then the glass reassembled.

Another variation in the environment box is Margaret Harper's interpretation of "environment" itself. Harper believes her box should both "contain and be composed of environmental materials" rather than as an environment for objects and the resulting microcosmic interpretation. She is interested in exploring the nature of materials and finds that the basic cube format is an excellent vehicle.

Howard Woody expands the box environment to include objects within and outside the box and to assemble the boxes themselves as sculpture. Cricket cages and birdcages were used ingeniously by some artists. Given the concept of an environment, several artists conceived of "boxlike" forms made from baskets and fibers in undulating, amoeboid shapes that contain suggestions of reality.

Steve Blumrich tapped nature's resources. His container is a seashell and within it is a magnificent mermaid made of sewn and stuffed batiked fabric. (See Color Section.)

The tin can serves as a dramatic and different container for the precious environments by Louis Goodman. Arthur Sandoval uses the can container for crocheted forms.

The possibilities of the small environment in a box, or another container, are as unlimited as the potential of our own lives in our larger environment.

UNTITLED BOXES. Margaret Harper. 1974. 8 inches high, 9 inches square. The artist is interested in exploring materials of the environment and incorporating them into a box form, which becomes a box environment. At left, bleached seaweed is poked through holes made in a box made of clear vinyl as shown in photo below at right. The natural seaweed is adhered to the vinyl box at right. Seaweed must be worked while it is wet.

THREAD AND SEAWEED. Margaret Harper. 1974. The box frame, made of welding rods with vinyl insets, remains partially exposed. Pieces of seaweed are attached to the vinyl with nylon thread. The natural dark seaweed has been bleached to lighten the color. Allow about 10 minutes in household bleach.

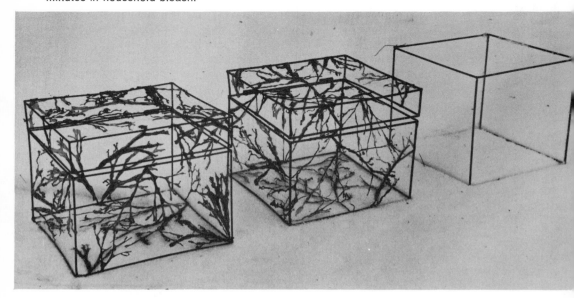

ENVIRONMENT IN A BOTTLE. Gordon Wagner. 1973. 22 inches high, 10 inches in diameter. Grass and assembled objects with cover.

THE INNER PERSON. Edward Higgins. 4½ inches high. Bronze casting.
Courtesy, artist

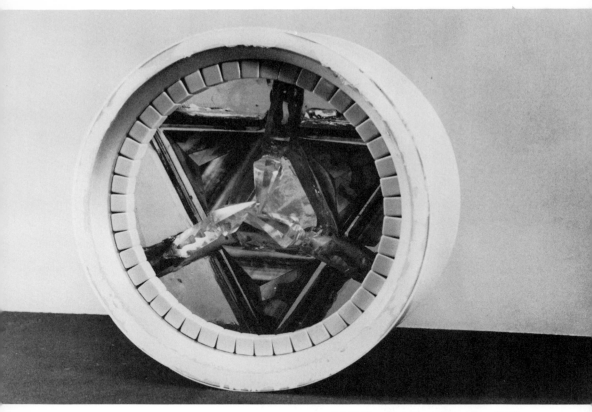

Z-14120. Christine Ziemnik. 1973. 9½ inches diameter, 4½ inches deep. A round form has been glassed in on both sides and within are repeat trapezoids with mirrors and glass crystals.

EGG BOX No. 2. John Henry. 1973. 20½ inches high, 9½ inches wide, 2¼ inches deep. A metal mechanic portion, with some of the fittings remaining, becomes the container for assembled objects including figures, eggs, straw.

Courtesy, artist

ANOTHER WORLD. Howard Woody. 1972. 26 inches high, 7 inches wide, 8 inches deep. Bubble gum machine, gum, bird nest, pigeon skeleton, prize capsules containing insects and doll parts, model of Statue of Liberty.

Courtesy, artist

A QUINTESSENT NOTION: BEGINNINGS AND ENDINGS. Amy Brown. 1973. 11½ inches high, 5 inches diameter. A bird's nest, eggs, and a raw fish spine sit in subjunction to Father Time. These organic elements have surrealist overtones; they are properly cushioned on a circle of amber fur.

Courtesy, artist

87

THE SAMENESS OF US ALL. Norma Minkowitz. 1974. 4 inches high, 9 inches wide; figures 2 inches each. Velvet box, crochet, hooking, beads, Dacron.

Courtesy, artist

KITTY PALACE. Sharon Sulentor. 1974. 20 inches high, 27 inches wide, 18 inches deep. Environment created of natural-color wool yarn, dyed sheep fleece, palm bark, jute braided coconut fiber, and leather. Fibers are crocheted, braided, and knotted to cover a wire armature.

Photo, Bill Sulentor

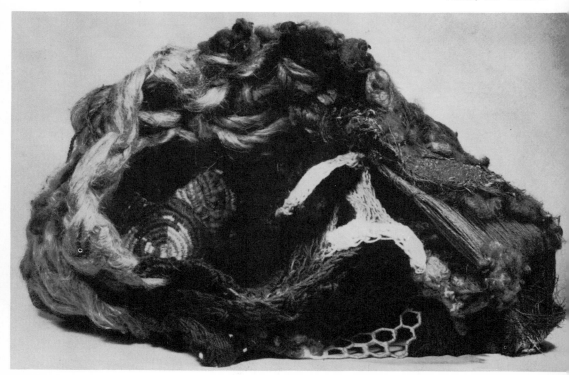

CANNED CLOUDS IN SKY SAUCE. Arthur A. Sandoval. 5½ inches high, 7 inches wide, 2½ inches deep. Gold plated container with crocheted Mylar and nylon. Some acrylic plastic. Nail polish is added as the "sauce" element. It is poured in three stages over the crocheted clouds: the first coat was a medium blue with glitter flakes, then a light blue pearlescent and finally a white pearlescent.

Photo, Charles H. Cox

TEA SERVICE. Sylvia Massey. 1974. 8 inches high, 14 inch triangle base. Terra-cotta and Plexiglas.

Courtesy, Jacqueline Anhalt Gallery, Los Angeles

NERD BIRD CAGE. Michael Sayers. 1974. Old bird cage, fibers, and feathers.

Courtesy, artist

SMALL MONUMENT III. Judith Citrin. 1972. 7½ inches high, 3¼ inches wide, 5 inches deep. Bamboo cricket cage, plastic soldiers, plaster, wood, enamel.

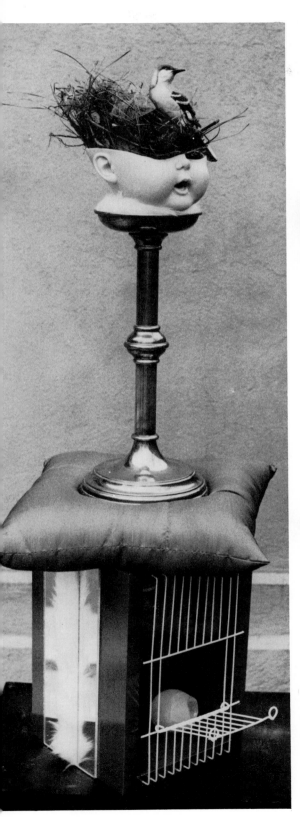

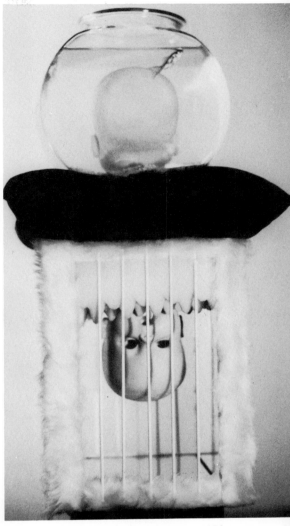

ALTERNATIVES.   Howard Woody.   1970.
23 inches high, 12 inches wide, 12 inches
deep.   Mirror covered wooden box, pillow, fish bowl, water, goldfish, dolls' heads,
bars, fur, foam rubber, fish gravel.
Courtesy, artist

IT'S ALL IN THE MIND.   Howard Woody.
36 inches high, 17 inches wide, 17 inches
deep.   Wooden box, pillow, candlestick
holder, doll face, bird nest, model bird,
mirror, fur, birdcage sections, feed swing,
light bulb fixture, broken light bulb, cast
resin broken light bulb.
Courtesy, artist

THE FLOOR CABINET. Hazel Janicki. 1972. 29¾ inches high, 14¼ inches wide, 10¾ inches deep. Found objects, tempera, modeling paste, wood panels.
Courtesy, artist

THE VIOLINIST. Arlene Seitzinger. 1973. Leather violin case, sculptured foam figure, found objects.

SOLDIERS. Antoni Miralda. 1968. Wood and plastic.
Courtesy, artist

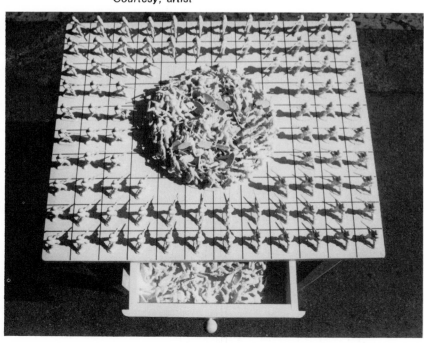

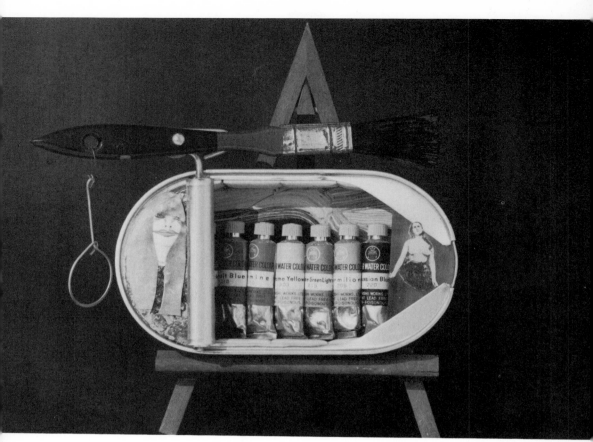

THE CAPTURED ARTIST. Louis Goodman. 1970.
7 inches high, 8 inches wide, 5 inches deep. Tubes
of paint in a sardine can set on a small easel. Collage and assemblage.
Collection, Dr. & Mrs. Mel Meilach, Chicago

ECOLOGICAL EVENT. Louis Goodman. 1970. 5
inches high, 4 inches wide, 2 inches deep. Collaged bottom of can with objects set in polyester
resin.
Collection, Dr. & Mrs. Mel Meilach, Chicago

Glue Chart

Materials to be glued	White glue	Resin glue	Polymer medium (acrylic emulsion)	Plastic resin urea base	Water-proof glue	Epoxy cement	Epoxy metal cement	House-hold glue	Contact cement	Rubber cement
Wood to wood	X	X		X	X					
Plastic to wood	X	X		X	X				X	
Wood outdoors				X	X					
Metal to wood	X	X				X	X		X	
China and glass						X		X		
Paper to paper and cardboard	X	X	X							X
Paper and cloth	X	X	X					X		
Cloth with wood	X	X	X					X		
Leather and wood	X	X	X						X	
Rubber to wood or metal						X	X	X	X	
Plastics, vinyls		X	X	X				X		
Collagraph items				X	X					
Glazing, preserving, sealing			X							
Stone and concrete to other items						X				
Rubber										X
Plastic foams		X	X	X				X	X	
Adding textures such as sand, stones, beads	X	X	X	X						
Metal to metal						X	X		X	

Always read and follow labels and manufacturers' directions.

Use of the glues as suggested in this chart is based on experience and knowledge, but it is not guaranteed. Individual experimentation with materials is recommended.

When gluing dissimilar materials, determine whether they are porous or non-porous. For example, porous materials are cloth, paper, cardboard, brick, wood and leather; non-porous materials are glass, metal, china, hard and soft plastics and rubber. Generally, when combining porous and non-porous materials, you should use the adhesive recommended for the non-porous material.

Selected Bibliography

Fraser, B. Kay. *Creative Bottle Cutting.* New York:
    Crown Publishers, 1972.

Hofsted, Jolyon S. *Step-by-Step Ceramics.* New York:
    Golden Press, 1967.

Lang, Nancy M. *Getting Started in Plastics.* New York:
    The Macmillan Company, 1972.

Meilach, Dona Z. *Creating Art from Anything.* Chicago:
    Henry Regnery, 1968.

Meilach, Dona Z. *Papier-Mâché Artistry.* New York:
    Crown Publishers, 1971.

Meilach, Dona Z., and Ten Hoor, Elvie. *Collage and Assemblage.*
    New York: Crown Publishers, 1973.

Newman, Jay H., and Newman, Lee Scott. *Plastics for the
    Craftsman.* New York: Crown Publishers, 1972.

Stribling, Mary Lou. *Art from Found Materials.* New York:
    Crown Publishers, 1970.

Index

C.P.: color pages